How To Make Spotted Dick

&

Other Suet Puddings

Geoff Wells

Authentic English Recipes
Book 10

Cover Artwork & Design by
Old Geezer Designs

Published in the United States by
Authentic English Recipes
an imprint of
DataIsland Software LLC,
Hollywood, Florida

https://ebooks.geezerguides.com

ISBN-13: 978-1482601596

ISBN-10: 1482601591

Table of Contents

DEDICATION

This series of books are dedicated to Mildred Ellen Wells 1906 - 2008

Mom lived for 102 incredible years. She went from horse drawn carriages and sailing ships to bullet trains and moon rockets.

She was not a fancy cook but everything she made tasted great. My dad grew much of what we ate in our garden so everything was always fresh and free of chemicals.

This book is a collection of some of her best recipes. I have just translated the quantities for the North American market.

I know she would be delighted to see all her recipes collected together so that you can continue to make these great tasting dishes.

Geoff Wells - Ontario, Canada - September 2012

INTRODUCTION

Spotted Dick is not the king of suet puddings but it certainly has the most memorable name - at least as far as North Americans are concerned.

Spotted Dicks are often the featured dessert items on British menus and it's not unusual to see many English men and women enjoying their Dicks covered in Bird's custard or Tate & Lyle's Golden Syrup.

FAQ's

What Is Suet?

The secret to making a great Spotted Dick is suet which is just a kind of fat.

Suet is the beef fat that surrounds the kidneys. It has a high melting point between 113°F and 122°F (45°C and 50°C). This is much higher than lard, (pork fat), which has a melting point between 86°F and 104°F (30°C and 40°C). Leaf fat lard, which is the highest grade, has a melting point between 109°F and 118°F (43°C and 48°C). Unfortunately leaf fat lard is rarely available commercially.

But I'm A Vegetarian

Not to worry, although true suet is made from animal fat you can buy a light version made entirely from vegetable fat. This is a commercial product made by Atora that can be used in any suet recipe.

Where Can I Buy Suet?

In Europe suet is readily available at any grocery store. I'm not sure about Australia but I imagine it is much like Canada where you can buy it if you ask the butcher to get it for you. In the US, where all the food is controlled by just a few giant corporations, you may have difficulty finding it in any store. Fortunately it is readily available online and you can find links at our web site https://authenticenglishrecipes.com

From The Butcher

If you are lucky enough to find a butcher that sells fresh suet you might be able to persuade him to prepare it for you - otherwise you can do it yourself.

Trim the pink connective tissue leaving just the pure white fat. Now chop the fat as finely as you can. Your butcher would run it through the meat grinder and if you have a home unit that would be perfect. A blender is not a good choice as you want the suet chopped not turned into a paste.

Substitutes for Suet

Real suet can be difficult to find in North America. If you are not able to obtain real suet you can substitute:

- ❖ the same amount of lard, frozen and shredded or
- ❖ the same amount of vegetable shortening, frozen and shredded or
- ❖ a package of Atora™ from Amazon
- ❖ http://amzn.to/2vXHD4d

What Is A Steamed Pudding?

As the name suggests a steamed pudding is cooked by steam rather than putting it in a dry oven. Usually, but not always, the pudding basin is lined with the suet crust, filled with meat or fruit, and closed with a suet crust top. The top is then covered with greasproof paper (wax or parchment paper is the closest US equivalent) and a cloth. Then the basin is lowered into a saucepan full of boiling water and cooked for about 3 hours.

What's A Pudding Cloth?

This is something cooks would fashion from an old bed sheet or similar material. It is laid on top of the pudding and tied under the lip of the basin with string. The four corners of the cloth are then raised on top and tied together. This provides a handle to remove the basin from the boiling water.

What Is A Pudding Basin?

If you go to our website you can see pictures of pudding basins which should make the idea clear. Basically it is a ceramic bowl with a lip around the edge. When you cover the top of your pudding with greasproof paper and a cloth you hold them on with a piece of string tied under the lip.

Typical Pudding Basin

MUST I USE A PUDDING BASIN?

No, a Spotted Dick is steamed without a basin but any meat or fruit pudding is cooked in a container. Any ceramic bowl or basin with a lip around the edge will work.

You can also make individual suet puddings in ramekins.

HOW MUCH COOKING WATER DO I USE?

Lower the basin into the saucepan containing about half a pot of water. The water level should be almost to the top of the basin but not covering it.

Bring the water to a boil and maintain the water level throughout the cooking process. Check every half hour or so and replenish any lost water by adding boiling water.

The saucepan should have a well fitting lid.

Self-Raising Flour

I think it is safe to say that most suet recipes you will find come from England, (most, not all). It's also a fair bet that many of those recipes will call for self-raising flour because that is more the norm than in North America. Even though self-raising flour is available in the US and Canada, North American recipes will typically specify all purpose flour. There is nothing magical about self-raising flour. It is just flour that has salt and leavening agents added.

To make your own self-raising flour just add 1½ teaspoons of baking powder and ¼ teaspoon of salt to 1 cup of all purpose flour. Make sure you mix it well.

Alternatively you can add one teaspoon of cream of tartar, ½ teaspoon of bicarbonate of soda and ¼ teaspoon of salt which will work just as well.

That being said all the recipes in this book are designed for the North American market and so use all purpose flour.

Obviously if you are in England and normally use self-raising flour just leave out the baking powder and salt from the suet crust recipes.

Measuring Ingredients

Most of the books in this series are more about the method and ingredients of the recipes rather than exact quantities. This book is a little different as it is all about baking and baking just won't work unless you get the chemistry right.

These are my mother's recipes, modified for the North American measuring system. I have also changed any reference to self-raising flour because it is not widely available here.

International Measurement Equivalents

While I'm talking about international differences I just want to mention that I've included metric measurement equivalents so you can make all the recipes no matter where in the world you live.

BASIC SUET CRUST

A suet crust is just a type of pastry but instead of baking it in an oven you boil or steam it. The result is more like a dumpling than a pie crust. In fact what I consider "real" dumplings are always made with suet. If you normally use Bisquik® for your dumplings give my suet dumpling recipe a try.

Suet pudding is a delicious English tradition found in both meat and fruit dishes. It can be eaten as is or covered with various toppings depending on if you are preparing an entrée or a dessert.

The basic recipe for a suet crust is 1 part suet to 1½ parts flour Since this is self-raising flour you will need to add 1½ teaspoons of baking powder and ¼ teaspoon of salt to every cup of all purpose flour.

A FEW TIPS

There are a few tips I want to share that will help make your suet puddings as good as they can be.

Start with your suet at room temperature. In other words take it out of the fridge an hour or so before you begin using it.

Suet pastry expands quite a bit as it cooks so be sure to allow for this. Fill pudding basins only two-thirds full to allow room for expansion.

Before cooking baked suet dishes, always make sure the oven is preheated to the correct temperature.

When steaming puddings make sure the water is boiling before the pudding is placed in the steamer or pan. Always top up the level with boiling water from a kettle.

HOW TO STEAM

Select a saucepan that is a little bit larger than your pudding basin. Half fill the saucepan with water and gentle lower your basin into the water. The water level should be just below the rim of the basin. Adjust the water level so that the boiling water will not spill on top of your pudding.

Use a tight fitting lid and adjust the water level every half hour.

Using a Steamer

A steamer works great for Spotted Dicks and Roly-polys. It's also a good choice if you make individual puddings in ramekins.

Using an Instant Pot

We now use an Instant Pot whenever we make a steamed pudding. It's just easier and more convenient.

It's much faster and we don't have to worry about the water level.

If you don' yet have an Instant Pot don't let that stop you from making these puddings but when you do get one be sure to try the Instant Pot methods that I have added.

Savoury Suet Pastry

Use this recipe for all your savoury meat and cheese puddings. Use ¾ of the dough to line the bottom and sides of your basin and the remaining ¼ for the pastry lid.

Ingredients

> 1½ cups (180g) flour
> 1 tablespoon (15 mL) baking powder
> ¾ teaspoon (4 mL salt
> ¼ teaspoon (1.25 mL) pepper
> 1 cup (125g) suet (see Page 3 for alternatives)
> 8 - 10 tablespoons (40-50 mL) cold water

Method

In a medium bowl, mix together the flour, baking powder, salt and pepper. Mix well with a fork to make sure the ingredients are well combined.

Cut in the suet, using a pastry blender, until the mixture looks like a coarse meal.

Trickle the cold water over the dry ingredients and mix with a fork until it begins to form a dough. Then, knead the dough until it is well formed and still a little sticky.

Sweet Suet Pastry

Use this recipe for all your sweet and fruit puddings. For filled fruit pudding use ¾ of the dough to line the bottom and sides of your basin and the remaining ¼ for the pastry lid.

If you're making a rolled pudding like a Spotted Dick or Roly-poly, roll the pastry to a rectangle approximately 8 inches by 12 inches. Add your filling and roll up to form an 8 inch finished length.

Ingredients

> 1½ cups (180 g) all purpose flour
> ⅓ cup (65g) sugar
> 1 tablespoon (15 mL) baking powder
> ¾ teaspoon (4 mL) salt
> 1 cup (125g) suet, finely chopped (see Page 3 for alternatives)
> 8 - 10 tablespoons (40-50 mL) milk

Method

In a medium bowl, mix together the flour, sugar, baking powder and salt. Mix well with a fork to make sure the ingredients are well combined.

Cut in the suet, using a pastry blender, until the mixture looks like a coarse meal.

Trickle the milk over the dry ingredients and mix with a fork until it begins to form a dough. Then, knead the dough until it is well formed and still a little sticky.

Spotted Dick

This recipe comes with a couple of suggested fillings. As long as you keep the measurements about the same, feel free to experiment with different types of fillings.

Ingredients

1 recipe sweet suet pastry (see Page 9)

Filling #1

¾ cup (115g) currants
1 small cooking apple, peeled, cored and diced
⅓ cup (60g) brown sugar
½ large lemon, zest only

Filling #2

¼ cup (40g) currants
¼ cup (40g) craisins (dried cranberries)
¼ cup (30g) walnuts
¼ cup (40g) dried mixed fruit
⅓ cup (60g) brown sugar, packed

Your Filling

It's okay to experiment. As long as you keep the quantities about the same you can mix up the filling ingredients. For example, I used raisins instead of currants, chopped almonds instead of walnuts, some chopped candied peel instead of the dried mix fruit … you get the idea.

METHOD

In a medium bowl, mix all the filling ingredients together making sure that the brown sugar is well distributed throughout the fruit and nuts. Set aside.

On a lightly floured surface, roll out the sweet suet pastry to form a rectangle approximately 8 inches by 12 inches (20 cm x 30 cm).

Evenly distribute the filling over the pastry and press the filling lightly into the pastry.

Roll up the pastry, as tightly as possible, from the smaller end. For example, start from the edge that is 8 inches (20 cm) wide so when you are finished you have a Spotted Dick that is 8 inches (20 cm) long.

Seal the ends and the seam by pinching them together.

Wrap the Spotted Dick in several layers of aluminum foil, twisting the ends to seal the package.

Steam the pudding for 2 hours.

Remove the completed Spotted Dick from the steamer and carefully unwrap. It will be very hot.

Slice off individual portions and serve with Tate & Lyle's Golden Syrup or Bird's dessert custard.

Servings: 6

SUET DUMPLINGS

Add dumplings to soups and stews during the last 10 - 20 minutes of cooking.

You can get creative and fill the centres with meat or cheese. Even boiling them in water and using them as a course on their own.

Try filling them with apples and raisins then cover with custard as a dessert.

INGREDIENTS

½ cup (120g) flour
¼ cup (30g) shredded <u>suet</u> (see Page 3 for alternatives)
¾ teaspoon (3.75 mL) baking powder
⅛ teaspoon (1.25 mL) salt
5 tablespoons (75 mL) cold water, approximately

METHOD

Put the flour, suet, baking powder and salt in a small bowl and mix well. Add just enough cold water to make the dough pliable but not sticky.

If it's too sticky add a little more flour.

Put a little flour on your hands and divide the dough into 8 pieces then roll them into balls.

About 10 - 20 minutes before your stew is done, drop the balls into the simmering liquid. Keep covered and cook gently until done. Turn them over half way through the process.

Servings: 4

SUGGESTIONS

You can add some interest by experimenting with various herbs added to your dough. Check out the Atora website for more dumpling recipes.

Apple and Blackberry Suet Pudding

This was my favorite fruit pudding combination but unfortunately I've never been able to find wild blackberries in North America with the intense flavour as those we used to pick on the common behind our house in England.

Ingredients

1 recipe sweet suet pastry (see page 9)

Filling

2 large cooking apples, cored, peel and sliced
1½ cups (190g) blackberries
⅓ cup (65g) sugar

Method

Roll out the sweet suet pastry and line a 1½ pint (700 mL) pudding basin with three-quarters of the pastry, reserving one-quarter for the lid.

In a medium bowl, toss together the apple slices, blackberries and sugar. Ladle the fruit and sugar mixture into the pastry-lined pudding basin.

Wet the edges of the pastry lid and then pinch the edges to seal the lid.

Cover the top of the pudding basin with waxed paper and a pudding cloth, tie securely with string and gather any excess pudding cloth over the top of the basin.

Steam for 2½ to 3 hours.

Serve with Bird's custard, heavy cream or ice cream.

Servings: 6

Suggestions

You can use many fruit combinations to make delicious puddings. Some of my favorite filings are plum, red and black currents, rhubarb, peach and gooseberry.

Carrot-Raisin Suet Pudding

This pudding is molded by the basin and turned out on a plate to serve. Cut generous slices and serve them with Bird's custard.

INGREDIENTS

2 medium carrots, coarsely grated
2 medium apples, peeled, cored and finely chopped
1 medium potato, peeled and finely chopped
1 cup (125g) suet, chopped (see Page 3 for alternatives)
1 cup (200g) sugar
⅓ cup (80 mL) orange juice
1 egg, beaten
1 teaspoon (5 mL) vanilla
1½ cups (180g) all purpose flour
1½ teaspoons (7.5 mL) baking soda
1 teaspoon (5 mL) cinnamon
1 teaspoon (5 mL) nutmeg, freshly grated
½ teaspoon (2.5 mL) ground cloves
½ teaspoon (2.5 mL) salt
1 cup (175g) dates, chopped
1 cup (150g) raisins

METHOD

Grease a 2 pint (950 mL) pudding basin.

In a large bowl, combine the carrots, apples, potato and suet. Mix well.

In a large measuring cup, combine the sugar, orange juice, egg, and vanilla. Mix well and stir into the carrot mixture.

In a medium bowl, combine the flour, baking soda, cinnamon, nutmeg, cloves, and salt. Mix well and stir into the carrot mixture.

Fold the dates and raisins into the carrot mixture.

Pour the batter into the greased pudding basin.

Cover the top of the basin with waxed paper and then a pudding cloth. Secure the pudding cloth with string and gather any excess cloth over the top.

Steam the pudding for 3½ hours.

Servings: 8

Christmas Plum Pudding

Traditionally our Christmas puddings contained several six-penny pieces but, although we all survived, this is not a tradition I would recommend.

INGREDIENTS

1¼ cups (150g) all purpose flour
½ teaspoon (2.5 mL) baking soda
1 teaspoon (5 mL) salt
1¼ cups (190g) Sultana raisins
1¼ cups (190g) seedless raisins
1 cup (150g) currants
1 cup (75g) mixed peel, chopped
1 cup (95g) maraschino cherries
1 cup (110g) blanched almonds, chopped
2 tablespoons (15g) all purpose flour
½ cup (115g) butter
1¼ cups (225g) brown sugar, firmly packed
4 eggs, beaten
2 tablespoons (30 mL) molasses
1½ cups (135g) dry bread crumbs
½ cup (120 mL) brandy
1 teaspoon (5 mL) cinnamon
½ teaspoon (2.5 mL) nutmeg
½ teaspoon (2.5 mL) ground cloves
1½ cups (185g) suet, finely chopped (see Page 3 for alternatives)
⅔ cup (160 mL) milk

METHOD

In a medium bowl or measuring cup, combine the flour, baking soda and salt. Set aside.

In a medium bowl, mix together the raisins, currants, peel, cherries, nuts and 2 tablespoons (15g) of flour. Toss well so that the flour coats all the other ingredients. Set aside.

In a large bowl cream together the butter and brown sugar until light and fluffy.

Beat the eggs well and add to the butter and sugar mixture. Then add the molasses, bread crumbs, brandy, spices and suet. Mix well.

Add in the floured fruit and nut mixture and mix well.

Add the flour, baking soda and salt mixture alternately with the milk and mix well.

Grease the pudding molds well and fill about 2/3rds full as the puddings will rise.

Cover with waxed paper and a pudding cloth tied with string.

Steam for 4 to 5 hours.

Serve warm.

Note: the pudding can be reheated by steaming for about 1½ to 2 hours.

Serve with a brandy or rum sauce which you can light just before bringing to the table. The flame maybe difficult to see unless you turn out the lights.

Servings: 8

Note: Christmas puddings are traditionally made months ahead and develop their flavour the longer you keep them.

Figgy Pudding

This is a very simple recipe for figgy pudding. It's fun to sometimes switch things around and serve a light entrée with the dessert as the feature.

Ingredients

¾ cup (95g) <u>suet</u> (see Page 3 for alternatives)
¾ cup (135g) brown sugar, packed
3 eggs
¼ cup (60 mL) cream sherry
1 cup (150g) figs, chopped
¼ cup (60 mL) molasses
1 teaspoon (5 mL) ground cinnamon
1½ cups (135g) dried bread crumbs
1 teaspoon (5 mL) vanilla

Method

Generously grease a 2 pint (950 mL) pudding basin and then coat with white sugar.

In a large bowl, combine the suet and brown sugar and mix well.

Add the eggs, vanilla and molasses and beat until well mixed.

Add the dried bread crumbs and cinnamon and mix until combined.

Add the cream sherry and mix just enough to make sure the sherry is well incorporated into the mixture.

Fold in the chopped figs.

> *Note: If you are using dried figs, rehydrate them by putting them in a small saucepan covered with water. Bring them to a boil, reduce heat and allow them to simmer for about 15 minutes. Pour off the excess liquid, allow the figs to cool and then coarsely chop them.*

Pour the completed batter into the prepared pudding basin. Cover the basin with some waxed paper and then a cloth. Tie with string and then lift the excess cloth over the top of the bowl and pin (this will be helpful when lifting the pudding in and out of the steaming pan).

Place the pudding in a pan large enough to hold the bowl with room left over. Fill the pan with hot water about three-quarters up the pudding basin. Cover the pan and bring the water to a boil over medium-high heat. Once the water is boiling, reduce heat to low and let the pudding steam for 3 hours.

Note: be sure to check the water every hour or so and add additional, boiling water as required.

When pudding is done, remove from basin and invert on a serving plate.

Serve warm with dessert custard.

Servings: 8

GINGER PUDDING

If you want to be really decadent you can warm some ginger marmalade and use that as a topping instead of the syrup.

INGREDIENTS

    1 cup (120g) all purpose flour
    1½ teaspoons (7.5 mL) ground ginger
    ¼ teaspoon (1.25 mL) baking soda
    ½ cup (120 mL) milk
    2 tablespoons (30 mL) Tate & Lyle's Golden Syrup
    2 tablespoons (30 mL) preserved ginger, chopped
    1 egg
    1½ cups (135g) bread crumbs
    1 tablespoon (15 mL) brown sugar
    1½ cups (190g) <u>suet</u> (see Page 3 for alternatives)

METHOD

In a small bowl, combine the flour, ground ginger and baking soda. Mix well and set aside.

In a small saucepan, heat the milk just to the simmering point, remove from heat and add the golden syrup and the beaten egg. Mix well.

> *Note: golden corn syrup may be substituted if you cannot get Tate & Lyle's Golden Syrup*

Stir in the bread crumbs, sugar, suet and chopped, preserved ginger. Add the flour mixture and stir to combine everything well.

Pour the completed mixture into a well greased 2 pint (950 mL) pudding basin.

Cover the top of the basin with waxed paper and then a pudding cloth. Secure the pudding cloth with string and gather any excess cloth over the top.

Steam the pudding for 2 hours.

Servings: 4

Jam Roly-Poly

This is a simple recipe that makes a wonderful dessert. It's very easy to make variations by changing the kind of jam or marmalade you use.

Ingredients

    1 recipe <u>sweet suet pastry</u> (see Page 9)
    5 - 6 tablespoons (75 - 90 mL) jam of your choice

Method

On a lightly floured surface, roll out the suet pastry to create a rectangle approximately 8 inches (20 cm) by 10 inches (25 cm).

Spread the rolled dough with the jam of your choice. The traditional choices are often raspberry or strawberry jam.

Spread the jam to about ½ an inch (1.25 cm) away from the edges.

Use some cold water to slightly wet the edges of the pastry. Then, roll up the pastry, from the shorter edge and seal the edges and seam.

Wrap the roly-poly well in 2 or 3 layers of aluminum foil and steam for 1 ½ hours.

Serve this dessert hot. Cut it into slices and serve with a dessert custard. It's also nice served with ice cream.

Baked Roly-Poly

This recipe can also be baked. In order to bake it, pre-heat your oven to 400°F (200°C, Gas Mark 6).

Coat a baking dish with non-stick cooking spray.

Bake at 400°F (200°C, Gas Mark 6) for 30-35 minutes, or until golden brown.

    Note: DO NOT wrap it in foil as you would for steaming.

Servings: 6

Leicestershire Pudding

This pudding is a good candidate to try as individual servings made in ramekins. Cook in a vegetable steamer for 1½ - 2 hours.

Ingredients

1½ cups (225g) raisins, seedless
1 cup (120g) all purpose flour
¾ cup (95g) suet, chopped (see Page 3 for alternatives)
2 eggs, beaten
1 teaspoon (5 mL) grated lemon peel
1 teaspoon (5 mL) nutmeg, freshly grated
2 tablespoons (30 mL) brandy
milk as needed

Method

Grease a 1½ pint (700 mL) pudding basin.

In a large bowl, combine the raisins, flour and suet and mix well. Mix together the raisins, flour and suet in a bowl.

Add the beaten eggs, lemon peel, nutmeg and brandy. Mix well.

Knead in enough milk to produce a firm dough and transfer the mixture into the greased pudding basin.

Cover with waxed paper and a pudding cloth tied with string.

Steam the pudding for 4 hours.

Serve with whipped cream or custard.

Servings: 6

LEMONY SUSSEX POND PUDDING

This pudding is from the county of Sussex and contains a whole lemon. During the long cooking time the lemon flavour infuses the butter and brown sugar which makes a thick lemon caramel.

Be sure to scrape out the centre of the lemon when you serve it. You can, of course, eat the candied skin if you wish.

Grocery store lemons are covered in wax so buy your lemons for this dish from an organic supplier.

INGREDIENTS

1 recipe sweet suet pastry (see Page 9)
zest of 1 lemon
½ cup (45g) breadcrumbs

FILLING

¾ cup (170g) cold butter, cut into small cubes
¾ cup (135g) brown sugar
1 large whole lemon, (this is a 2nd lemon with the skin intact)

METHOD

Start by adding the zest of one lemon and the breadcrumbs to the sweet suet pastry recipe.

Grease a 1½ quart (1.5 L) pudding basin.

Roll out the sweet suet pastry and line the pudding basin with the pastry. Reserve enough pastry to make a lid for after you have filled the pudding.

Put the lemon on a hard surface and roll your hand over it. This will help to release the juice. Prick the lemon all over with a fork or toothpick then add half the sugar, butter and whole lemon to the centre of the pudding. Place the remaining sugar and butter around the edge of the lemon.

Wet the edges of the suet pastry lid and place on top. Pinch the edges to seal.

Cover the top of the basin with waxed paper and then a pudding cloth. Secure the pudding cloth with string and gather any excess cloth over the top.

Steam the pudding for 3 hours.

Serve with custard, heavy cream or ice cream.

Servings: 6

MIDDLESEX POND PUDDING

You will notice that this is very similar to the previous recipe for the Sussex Pond Pudding. Middlesex is the county I was born in so, as this was my variation, I named it thus but this is the only place you will find anything called a Middlesex Pond Pudding.

INGREDIENTS

 1 recipe <u>sweet suet pastry</u> (see Page 9)
 zest of ½ orange
 ½ cup (45g) breadcrumbs

FILLING

 1 small lemon, thinly sliced
 1 small lime, thinly sliced
 1 small orange, thinly sliced
 2 tablespoons (15g) all purpose flour

¾ cup (135g) brown sugar

½ cup (150g) cold butter, cut into small cubes

METHOD

Grease a 1½ quart (700 mL) pudding basin.

Roll out the sweet suet pastry and line the pudding basin with the pastry. Reserve enough pastry to make a lid for after you have filled the pudding.

In a medium bowl toss the lemon, lime and orange slices with the 2 tablespoons (15g) of all purpose flour.

To make the filling, create layers starting with 2 tablespoons (25g) of the brown sugar, 3 or 4 cubes of butter and a few slices of lemon, lime and orange. Continue with these layers until you've used up all of the filling ingredients.

Wet the edges of the suet pastry lid and place on top. Pinch the edges to seal.

Cover the top of the basin with waxed paper and then a pudding cloth. Secure the pudding cloth with string and gather any excess cloth over the top.

Steam the pudding for 3 hours.

Servings: 6

TREACLE PUDDING

If you have a sweet tooth you'll be sure to like this. Like the Leicestershire Pudding this works well as individual servings made in ramekins. Cook in a vegetable steamer for about an hour.

INGREDIENTS

¼ cup (60 mL) dark treacle, substitute molasses if you can't find treacle
¼ cup (60 mL) Tate & Lyle's golden syrup, substitute corn syrup if you can't find Tate & Lyle's
¼ teaspoon (1.25 mL) cinnamon
2 cups (240g) all purpose flour
3 teaspoons (15 mL) baking powder
1 cup (125g) <u>suet</u>, finely chopped (see Page 3 for alternatives)
⅓ cup (60g) brown sugar
⅓ cup (65g) white sugar
⅔ cup (160 mL) milk
2 eggs, beaten

METHOD

Grease a 1½ pint (700 mL) pudding basin.

Note: make sure to grease the basin well or the treacle might stick.

Pour the treacle and golden syrup into the base of the pudding basin.

In a medium bowl combine the flour, cinnamon and baking powder and mix well. Cut in the suet with a pastry blender until the mixture resembles a coarse meal.

Add both the white and brown sugar to the flour mixture and stir well.

In a medium bowl, combine the milk and beaten eggs.

Slowly pour the egg mixture into the flour mixture and stir until all ingredients are well combined and make a soft, sticky dough.

Carefully spoon the dough into the pudding basin being careful not to disturb the treacle too much.

Cover the top of the basin with waxed paper and then a pudding cloth. Secure the pudding cloth with string and gather any excess cloth over the top.

Steam the pudding for 2 hours.

Allow the pudding to cool on a wire rack for 5 minutes and then turn the pudding out on a plate, allowing the treacle to dribble down the sides.

Servings: 6

Bonus Recipe - Mincemeat

I have included a mincemeat recipe because mincemeat is made with suet. Commercial mincemeat is surprisingly expensive and not nearly as good as homemade. This recipe is for a small quantity that you would use for a pie. If you wish you can make a big batch and store it for a year or more.

You should make it at least two weeks before you plan to use it so that the flavours have a chance to mature.

Ingredients

1 cup (125g) finely chopped beef <u>suet</u> (see Page 3 for alternatives)
2 granny smith apples, unpeeled, cored and finely chopped
1 cup (150g) raisins
¾ cup (115g) currants
½ cup (75g) sultanas
½ cup (90g) packed dark brown sugar
¼ cup (20g) candied peel (lemon/orange)
zest and juice of ½ a fresh lemon
zest and juice of one orange
1½ teaspoons (7.5 mL) freshly grated nutmeg
½ teaspoon (2.5 mL) ground cloves
¼ teaspoon (1.25 mL) mace
½ teaspoon (2.5 mL) cinnamon
¼ cup (60 mL)brandy or dark rum

Method

In a bowl, combine everything except the brandy or rum. Mix well.

Transfer the mixture to a saucepan and heat until the suet has completely melted and the mixture is heated through.

Remove from heat, cool, then stir in the brandy. Pack into a 2 - 2 cup (475 mL) jars and refrigerate.

Of course if you properly sterilize and seal your jars the mincemeat will keep for years without refrigeration. After all mincemeat was originally a way to preserve meat.

Cheese and Leek Suet Pudding

I've always thought that leeks are a much under used vegetable. Try these next two recipes for something a little different.

Ingredients

    1 recipe <u>savoury suet pastry</u> (see Page 8)

Filling

    3 tablespoons (40g) butter
    1 pound (450g) leeks
    2 tablespoons (15g) all purpose flour
    1 cup (100g) sharp cheddar cheese, shredded
    ¼ cup (60 mL) water
    1 teaspoon (5 mL) dried thyme
    sea salt, to taste
    freshly ground black pepper, to taste

Method

Cut the leeks in half, lengthwise and clean well. Remove the tougher green pieces and slice.

In a large skillet, melt the butter over low heat and add the leeks. Cook for about 10 minutes or until soft. Sprinkle the flour over the leeks, mix well and continue to cook, over low heat, for another 2 minutes.

Slowly add the milk, stirring constantly. Then add the grated cheese and stir well to combine.

When the mixture begins to thicken, remove from heat and stir in the salt and pepper to taste. Set aside and allow the mixture to cool completely.

Once the cheese and leek filling has cooled, grease a 2 pint (950 mL) pudding basin, roll out the suet pastry and line the pudding basin with the pastry. Ladle the filling into the basin and then cover with a pastry lid.

Cover the top of the basin with waxed paper and then a pudding cloth. Secure the pudding cloth with string and gather any excess cloth over the top.

Steam the pudding for 2 hours.

Servings: 4

Ham and Leek Suet Pudding

After you have tried these two leek recipes, why not combine them for a third variation.

Ingredients

1 recipe <u>savoury suet pastry</u> (see Page 8)

Filling

12 ounces (340g) cooked ham
1 leek
1½ tablespoons (25g) butter
1½ tablespoons (11g) all purpose flour
1 cup (240 mL) chicken stock
2 sprigs fresh thyme
pepper, to taste

Method

Cut the cooked ham into small cubes. Wash the leek well and remove the tough green top of the leek. Then cut the leek into thin slices.

In a medium saucepan, melt the butter over medium heat and cook the leek slices until tender. Sprinkle the flour over the leeks and stir well.

Slowly add the hot chicken stock, stirring constantly. Continue stirring, over medium heat, until the mixture comes to a boil and begins to thicken.

Reduce heat and add the thyme, cream and ham.

Stir well and simmer for about 5 minutes.

Remove from heat and set aside to cool.

Once the ham and leek filling has cooled, grease a 2 pint (950 mL) pudding basin, roll out the suet pastry and line the pudding basin with the pastry. Ladle the filling into the basin and then cover with a pastry lid.

Cover the top of the basin with waxed paper and then a pudding cloth. Secure the pudding cloth with string and gather any excess cloth over the top.

Steam the pudding for 2 hours.

Servings: 4

Steak and Kidney Pudding

Of all the meals I enjoyed growing up this was my favorite. I truly believe there isn't a better tasting meal to be had. Please try it at least once, exactly as I present it.

I know how Americans gag at the thought of eating kidney but before you do check out what goes into a hot dog.

If you really can't bring yourself to try it leave it in large pieces and remove it before serving. This way you at least get the benefit of the flavour in your gravy. Trust me - this will be the best gravy you have ever tasted.

Ingredients

    1 recipe <u>savoury suet pastry</u> (see Page 8)

Filling

    3 - 4 lb (1.3 - 1.8 Kg) blade or top sirloin roast
    ⅓ beef kidney
    1 large onion
    4 medium carrots
    ½ teaspoon (2.5 mL) salt
    2 tablespoons (30 mL) of Bovril™
    2 tablespoons (15g) corn starch

Method

Cut the roast into 1 inch (2.5 cm) cubes and be sure to remove any fat, skin or gristle. Cut the kidney into bite size pieces or ½ dozen pieces if you don't plan to eat it.

Put the cubes in a large saucepan with a heavy bottom. Over a fairly high heat toss the cubes around in the saucepan until all the meat is seared and no red is visible.

Add cold water until the water is almost at the level of the meat. DO NOT add too much water, it will dilute the taste.

Chop the onion and add it to the pot. Peel the carrots and chop them into 1 inch (2.5 cm) pieces. Add them to the pot. Add the Bovril™.

Bring the beef mixture to a simmer and cook for 30 minutes or until the carrots are just starting to soften. Remove from heat and drain the gravy into another saucepan. Don't overcook it.

Mix the cornstarch with just enough water to make a thin paste. Use as little water as possible to make the cornstarch workable.

Bring the gravy to a simmer and slowly add the cornstarch until the gravy is the consistency of cooking oil.

Once the beef and kidney filling has cooled, grease a 2 pint (950 mL) pudding basin, roll out the suet pastry and line the pudding basin with the pastry. Ladle the filling into the basin and add ¼ cup (60 mL) of the gravy.

Don't add hot filling to the pastry as it will make it mushy.

Cover the meat with a pastry lid then cover the top of the basin with waxed paper and then a pudding cloth. Secure the pudding cloth with string and gather any excess cloth over the top.

Steam the pudding for 2 hours.

Serve the pudding with the rest of the gravy (reheated separately), boiled potatoes and fresh peas or scarlet runner beans.

Servings: 6 - 8

Personal note

Tastes vary but for me the pastry at the bottom of the bowl has just about the most wonderful flavour you can imagine. Pour as much gravy as you can into the pudding as you serve. This way it has a chance to soak in and flavour the crust.

~~~

Air Fryer & Instant Pot Methods

I guess when it comes to these new fangled gadgets, we're a little late to the party, but they have now found an important place in my and Vicky's kitchen.

We use these new appliances so much we decided to re-release the Authentic English Recipes series with Air Fryer and Instant Pot directions for all appropriate recipes.

We have also added video's for all these recipes to our

https://instantpotvideorecipes.com

membership site.

As one of our loyal readers you get a free membership to this site as a bonus for buying this book. All you do is visit the secret claim page to get your 100% discount coupon code.

https://fun.geezerguides.com/freemembership

Instant Pot Steamed Puddings

I love steamed puddings, in fact steak and kidney pudding is probably my most favorite meal of all. And my wife and I are now mostly vegetarian. I'm not worried about the suet but we do try to avoid eating meat most of the time.

One of the drawbacks to eating a steamed pudding is that they are a bit of a pain to cook. You have to keep a close eye on the water level in case you run out or overflow the basin.

The Instant Pot eliminates this drawback and makes cooking suet puddings very easy. They are still not diet food but they certainly make for an occasional treat and are sure to be a hit with your dinner party guest who have probably never tried one before.

To make things easy for you I am repeating most of the recipes in this book but with Instant pot directions.

INSTANT POT SPOTTED DICK

There are many recipes around for Spotted Dick and some of them suggest you make this recipe in a basin, like other steamed puddings. However, that is NOT a traditional Spotted Dick.

This recipe is for a traditional Spotted Dick cooked in a non-traditional way - in an Instant Pot! And that's the only way this recipe differs from the traditional recipe.

INGREDIENTS

1 recipe <u>sweet suet pastry</u> (see Page 9)

FILLING #1 - (CHOOSE FILLING #1 OR FILLING #2)

¾ cup (115g) currants
1 small cooking apple, peeled, cored and diced
⅓ cup (60g) brown sugar
½ large lemon, zest only

FILLING #2 - (CHOOSE FILLING #1 OR FILLING #2)

¼ cup (40g) currants
¼ cup (40g) craisins (dried cranberries)
¼ cup (30g) walnuts
¼ cup (40g) dried mixed fruit
⅓ cup (60g) brown sugar, packed

YOUR FILLING

It's okay to experiment. As long as you keep the quantities about the same you can mix up the filling ingredients. For example, I used raisins instead of currants, chopped almonds instead of walnuts, some chopped candied peel instead of the dried mix fruit … you get the idea.

METHOD

In a medium bowl, mix all the filling ingredients together making sure that the brown sugar is well distributed throughout the fruit and nuts. Set aside.

On a lightly floured surface, roll out the sweet suet pastry to form a rectangle approximately 6½ to 7 inches (16.5 to 17.5 cm) by 10 to 11 inches (25 to 28 cm).

Evenly distribute the filling over the pastry and press the filling lightly into the pastry.

Roll up the pastry, as tightly as possible, from the smaller end. For example, start from the edge that is 6½ to 7 inches (16.5 to 17.5 cm) wide so when you are finished you have a Spotted Dick that is 6½ to 7 inches (16.5 to 17.5 cm) long.

Seal the ends and the seam by pinching them together.

Wrap the Spotted Dick well in 2 or 3 layers of aluminum foil and twist the ends to seal.

Place the trivet in the inner liner and pour in 2 cups (480 mL) of boiling water.

Carefully place the foil-wrapped pudding on the trivet.

Close and lock the lid of the Instant Pot, ensuring the Pressure Valve is in the Sealing position.

Select the Steam function and set the cooking time for 45 minutes.

Once cooking time is complete allow for a complete Natural Pressure Release (Wait for the float valve to drop on it's own. This can take up to 45 minutes.)

Remove the completed Spotted Dick from the Instant Pot and allow to cool on a wire rack for 5-10 minutes.

Carefully remove the aluminum foil and slice into serving portions.

Serve with Tate & Lyle's Golden Syrup or Bird's custard.

Instant Pot Apple and Blackberry Pudding

Ingredients

1 recipe sweet suet pastry (see Page 9)

Filling

2 large cooking apples, cored, peel and sliced
1½ cups (190g) blackberries
⅓ cup (65g) sugar

Method

Roll out the sweet suet pastry and line a 1½ pint (700 mL) pudding basin (note: make sure the pudding basin will fit properly in your Instant Pot) with three-quarters of the pastry, reserving one-quarter for the lid.

In a medium bowl, toss together the apple slices, blackberries and sugar. Ladle the fruit and sugar mixture into the pastry-lined pudding basin.

Wet the edges of the pastry lid and then pinch the edges to seal the lid.

Cover the top of the pudding basin with parchment paper or aluminum foil and a pudding cloth. Tie the pudding cloth securely with string and gather any excess pudding cloth over the top of the basin. Note: The pudding cloth is optional, however, you need to make sure that no water gets into the basin while it's steaming. I like to use a pudding cloth because that's the way I've always done it. And, it makes it easier to get the pudding into and out of the pot.

Place the trivet in the stainless steel liner of the Instant Pot.

Add approximately 6 cups (1.4 L) of boiling water to the inner pot (This worked perfect for the basin I used in a 6-quart Instant Pot. The goal is to have the water be about 1" (2.5 cm) below the rim of the pudding basin. Adjust the amount of boiling water to suit your pot and basin.)

Gently lower the prepared pudding basin onto the trivet. Check the water level in relation to the pudding basin and adjust if necessary.

Close and lock the lid of the Instant Pot, ensuring the Pressure Valve is in the Sealing position.

Select the Steam function and set the cooking time for 90 minutes.

Once cooking time is complete allow for a complete Natural Pressure Release (Wait for the float valve to drop on it's own. This can take up to 45 minutes.)

Remove the completed pudding from the Instant Pot and carefully remove the pudding cloth and parchment paper or aluminum foil.

Allow the pudding to cool for 10-15 minutes.

Invert on a serving dish, if desired.

Serve with Bird's custard, heavy cream or ice cream.

Instant Pot Carrot-Raisin Pudding

Ingredients

    2 medium carrots, coarsely grated
    2 medium apples, peeled, cored and finely chopped
    1 medium potato, peeled and finely chopped
    1 cup (125g) suet, chopped (see Page 3 for alternatives)
    1 cup (200g) sugar
    ⅓ cup (80 mL) orange juice
    1 egg, beaten
    1 teaspoon (5 mL) vanilla
    1½ cups (180g) all purpose flour
    1½ teaspoons (7.5 mL) baking soda
    1 teaspoon (5 mL) cinnamon
    1 teaspoon (5 mL) nutmeg, freshly grated
    ½ teaspoon (2.5 mL) ground cloves
    ½ teaspoon (2.5 mL) salt
    1 cup (175g) dates, chopped
    1 cup (150g) raisins

Method

Grease a 2 pint (950 mL) pudding basin (note: make sure the pudding basin will fit properly in your Instant Pot).

In a large bowl, combine the carrots, apples, potato and suet. Mix well.

In a large measuring cup, combine the sugar, orange juice, egg, and vanilla. Mix well and stir into the carrot mixture.

In a medium bowl, combine the flour, baking soda, cinnamon, nutmeg, cloves, and salt. Mix well and stir into the carrot mixture.

Fold the dates and raisins into the carrot mixture.

Pour the batter into the greased pudding basin.

Cover the top of the pudding basin with parchment paper or aluminum foil and a pudding cloth. Tie the pudding cloth securely with string and gather any excess pudding cloth over the top of the basin. Note: The pudding cloth is optional, however, you need to make sure that no water gets into the basin while it's steaming. I like to use a pudding cloth because that's the way I've always done it. And, it makes it easier to get the pudding into and out of the pot.

Place the trivet in the stainless steel liner of the Instant Pot.

Add approximately 6 cups (1.4 L) of boiling water to the inner pot (This worked perfect for the basin I used in a 6-quart Instant Pot. The goal is to have the water be about 1" (2.5 cm) below the rim of the pudding basin. Adjust the amount of boiling water to suit your pot and basin.)

Gently lower the prepared pudding basin onto the trivet. Check the water level in relation to the pudding basin and adjust if necessary.

Close and lock the lid of the Instant Pot, ensuring the Pressure Valve is in the Sealing position.

Select the Steam function and set the cooking time for 120 minutes.

Once cooking time is complete allow for a complete Natural Pressure Release (Wait for the float valve to drop on it's own. This can take up to 45 minutes.)

Remove the completed pudding from the Instant Pot and carefully remove the pudding cloth and parchment paper or aluminum foil.

Allow the pudding to cool for 10-15 minutes.

Invert on a serving dish, if desired.

Serve with Bird's custard, heavy cream or ice cream.

INSTANT POT CHRISTMAS PLUM PUDDING

This recipe makes a lot - enough for 4 to 6 steamed puddings depending on the size of basin (bowl) you choose to use - 1½ or 2 pint (700 or 900 mL). You'll need to cook each one individually in the Instant Pot.

INGREDIENTS

    1¼ cups (150g) all purpose flour
    ½ teaspoon (2.5 mL) baking soda
    1 teaspoon (5 mL) salt
    1¼ cups (190g) Sultana raisins
    1¼ cups (190g) seedless raisins
    1 cup (150g) currants
    1 cup (75g) mixed peel, chopped
    1 cup (95g) maraschino cherries
    1 cup (110g) blanched almonds, chopped
    2 tablespoons (15g) all purpose flour
    ½ cup (115g) butter
    1¼ cups (225g) brown sugar, firmly packed
    4 eggs, beaten
    2 tablespoons (30 mL) molasses
    1½ cups (135g) dry bread crumbs
    ½ cup (120 mL) brandy
    1 teaspoon (5 mL) cinnamon
    ½ teaspoon (2.5 mL) nutmeg
    ½ teaspoon (2.5 mL) ground cloves
    1½ cups (185g) suet, finely chopped (see Page 3 for alternatives)
    ⅔ cup (160 mL) milk

METHOD

In a medium bowl or measuring cup, combine the flour, baking soda and salt. Set aside.

In a medium bowl, mix together the raisins, currants, peel, cherries, nuts and 2 tablespoons (15g) of flour. Toss well so that the flour coats all the other ingredients. Set aside.

In a large bowl cream together the butter and brown sugar until light and fluffy.

Beat the eggs well and add to the butter and sugar mixture. Then add the molasses, bread crumbs, brandy, spices and suet. Mix well.

Add in the floured fruit and nut mixture and mix well.

Add the flour, baking soda and salt mixture alternately with the milk and mix well.

Grease the pudding molds well and fill about 2/3rds full as the puddings will rise.

Cover the top of the pudding basin with parchment paper or aluminum foil and a pudding cloth. Tie the pudding cloth securely with string and gather any excess pudding cloth over the top of the basin.

> *Note: The pudding cloth is optional, however, you need to make sure that no water gets into the basin while it's steaming. I like to use a pudding cloth because that's the way I've always done it. And, it makes it easier to get the pudding into and out of the pot.*

Place the trivet in the stainless steel liner of the Instant Pot.

Add approximately 6 cups (1.4 L) of boiling water to the inner pot (This worked perfect for the basin I used in a 6-quart Instant Pot. The goal is to have the water be about 1" (2.5 cm) below the rim of the pudding basin. Adjust the amount of boiling water to suit your pot and basin.)

Gently lower the prepared pudding basin onto the trivet.

Check the water level in relation to the pudding basin and adjust if necessary.

Close and lock the lid of the Instant Pot, ensuring the Pressure Valve is in the Sealing position.

Select the Steam function and set the cooking time for 45 minutes.

Once cooking time is complete allow for a complete Natural Pressure Release (Wait for the float valve to drop on it's own. This can take up to 45 minutes.)

Remove the completed pudding from the Instant Pot and carefully remove the pudding cloth and parchment paper or aluminum foil.

Allow the pudding to cool for 10-15 minutes.

You can turn the pudding out at this point and allow it to continue cooling while you start the next on in your instant pot.

Tip: If you have more than one basin, you can be preparing the next one while the previous one is cooking.

Serve with a brandy or rum sauce which you can light just before bringing to the table. The flame may be difficult to see unless you turn out the lights.

> Tip: The pudding can be reheated by steaming for about 8 to 10 minutes in the Instant Pot. Follow the directions given above and reduce the cooking time to 10 minutes.

> Tip: These puddings will freeze well. Wrap in two layers of waxed paper and then in aluminum foil. Allow to thaw at room temperature when you remove them from the freezer.

Instant Pot Figgy Pudding

Ingredients

¾ cup (95g) <u>suet</u> (see Page 3 for alternatives)
¾ cup (135g) brown sugar, packed
3 eggs
¼ cup (60 mL) cream sherry
1 cup (150g) figs, chopped
¼ cup (60 mL) molasses
1 teaspoon (5 mL) ground cinnamon
1½ cups (135g) dried bread crumbs
1 teaspoon (5 mL) vanilla

Method

Generously grease a 2 pint (950 mL) pudding basin and then coat with white sugar.

In a large bowl, combine the suet and brown sugar and mix well.

Add the eggs, vanilla and molasses and beat until well mixed.

Add the dried bread crumbs and cinnamon and mix until combined.

Add the cream sherry and mix just enough to make sure the sherry is well incorporated into the mixture.

Fold in the chopped figs.

> *Note: If you are using dried figs, rehydrate them by putting them in a small saucepan covered with water. Bring them to a boil, reduce heat and allow them to simmer for about 15 minutes. Pour off the excess liquid, allow the figs to cool and then coarsely chop them.*

Pour the completed batter into the prepared pudding basin.

Cover the top of the pudding basin with parchment paper or aluminum foil and a pudding cloth. Tie the pudding cloth securely with string and gather any excess pudding cloth over the top of the basin. Note: The pudding cloth is optional, however, you need to make sure that no water gets into the basin while it's steaming. I like to use a pudding cloth because that's the way I've always done it. And, it makes it easier to get the pudding into and out of the pot.

Place the trivet in the stainless steel liner of the Instant Pot.

Add approximately 6 cups (1.4 L) of boiling water to the inner pot (This worked perfect for the basin I used in a 6-quart Instant Pot. The goal is to have the water be about 1" (2.5 cm) below the rim of the pudding basin. Adjust the amount of boiling water to suit your pot and basin.)

Gently lower the prepared pudding basin onto the trivet. Check the water level in relation to the pudding basin and adjust if necessary.

Close and lock the lid of the Instant Pot, ensuring the Pressure Valve is in the Sealing position.

Select the Steam function and set the cooking time for 90 minutes.

Once cooking time is complete allow for a complete Natural Pressure Release (Wait for the float valve to drop on it's own. This can take up to 45 minutes.)

Remove the completed pudding from the Instant Pot and carefully remove the pudding cloth and parchment paper or aluminum foil.

Allow the pudding to cool for 10-15 minutes.

Invert on a serving dish, if desired.

Serve with Bird's custard, heavy cream or ice cream.

INSTANT POT GINGER PUDDING

INGREDIENTS

1 cup (120g) all purpose flour
1½ teaspoons (7.5 mL) ground ginger
¼ teaspoon (1.25 mL) baking soda
½ cup (120 mL) milk
2 tablespoons (30 mL) Tate & Lyle's Golden Syrup
2 tablespoons (30 mL) preserved ginger, chopped
1 egg
1½ cups (135g) bread crumbs
1 tablespoon (15 mL) brown sugar
1½ cups (190g) suet (see Page 3 for alternatives)

METHOD

In a small bowl, combine the flour, ground ginger and baking soda. Mix well and set aside.

In a small saucepan, heat the milk just to the simmering point, remove from heat and add the golden syrup and the beaten egg. Mix well.

Note: golden corn syrup may be substituted if you cannot get Tate & Lyle's Golden Syrup

Stir in the bread crumbs, sugar, suet and chopped, preserved ginger. Add the flour mixture and stir to combine everything well.

Pour the completed mixture into a well greased 2 pint (950 mL) pudding basin.

Cover the top of the pudding basin with parchment paper or aluminum foil and a pudding cloth. Tie the pudding cloth securely with string and gather any excess pudding cloth over the top of the basin. Note: The pudding cloth is optional, however, you need to make sure that no water gets into the basin while it's steaming. I like to use a pudding cloth because that's the way I've always done it. And, it makes it easier to get the pudding into and out of the pot.

Place the trivet in the stainless steel liner of the Instant Pot.

Add approximately 6 cups (1.4 L) of boiling water to the inner pot (This worked perfect for the basin I used in a 6-quart Instant Pot. The goal is to have the water be about 1" (2.5 cm) below the rim of the pudding basin. Adjust the amount of boiling water to suit your pot and basin.)

Gently lower the prepared pudding basin onto the trivet. Check the water level in relation to the pudding basin and adjust if necessary.

Close and lock the lid of the Instant Pot, ensuring the Pressure Valve is in the Sealing position.

Select the Steam function and set the cooking time for 60 minutes.

Once cooking time is complete allow for a complete Natural Pressure Release (Wait for the float valve to drop on it's own. This can take up to 45 minutes or more.)

Remove the completed pudding from the Instant Pot and carefully remove the pudding cloth and parchment paper or aluminum foil.

Allow the pudding to cool for 10-15 minutes.

Invert on a serving dish, if desired.

Serve with Bird's custard, heavy cream or ice cream.

Instant Pot Jam Roly-Poly

Ingredients

1 recipe <u>sweet suet pastry</u> (see Page 9)

5 - 6 tablespoons (75 - 90 mL) jam of your choice

Method

On a lightly floured surface, roll out the suet pastry to create a rectangle approximately 6½ to 7 inches (16.5 to 17.5 cm) by 10 to 11 inches (25 to 28 cm). (It needs to be sized to fit into the inner liner of your Instant Pot.)

Spread the rolled dough with the jam of your choice. The traditional choices are often raspberry or strawberry jam.

Spread the jam to about ½ an inch (1.25 cm) away from the edges.

Use some cold water to slightly wet the edges of the pastry. Then, roll up the pastry, from the shorter edge and seal the edges and seam.

Wrap the roly-poly well in 2 or 3 layers of aluminum foil and twist the ends to seal.

Place the trivet in the inner liner and pour in 2 cups (480 mL) of boiling water.

Carefully place the foil-wrapped pudding on the trivet.

Close and lock the lid of the Instant Pot, ensuring the Pressure Valve is in the Sealing position.

Select the Steam function and set the cooking time for 45 minutes.

Once cooking time is complete allow for a complete Natural Pressure Release (Wait for the float valve to drop on it's own. This can take up to 45 minutes.)

Remove the completed Roly-Poly from the Instant Pot and allow to cool on a wire rack for 5-10 minutes.

Carefully remove the aluminum foil and slice into serving portions.

Serve with Bird's custard, heavy cream or ice cream.

Instant Pot Leicestershire Pudding

Ingredients

    1½ cups (225g) raisins, seedless
    1 cup (120g) all purpose flour
    ¾ cup (95g) <u>suet</u>, chopped (see Page 3 for alternatives)
    2 eggs, beaten
    1 teaspoon (5 mL) grated lemon peel
    1 teaspoon (5 mL) nutmeg, freshly grated
    2 tablespoons (30 mL) brandy
    milk

Method

Grease a 1½ pint (700 mL) pudding basin.

In a large bowl, combine the raisins, flour and suet and mix well. Mix together the raisins, flour and suet in a bowl.

Add the beaten eggs, lemon peel, nutmeg and brandy. Mix well.

Knead in enough milk to produce a firm dough and transfer the mixture into the greased pudding basin.

Cover the top of the pudding basin with parchment paper or aluminum foil and a pudding cloth. Tie the pudding cloth securely with string and gather any excess pudding cloth over the top of the basin. Note: The pudding cloth is optional, however, you need to make sure that no water gets into the basin while it's steaming. I like to use a pudding cloth because that's the way I've always done it. And, it makes it easier to get the pudding into and out of the pot.

Place the trivet in the stainless steel liner of the Instant Pot.

Add approximately 6 cups (1.4 L) of boiling water to the inner pot (This worked perfect for the basin I used in a 6-quart Instant Pot. The goal is to have the water be about 1" (2.5 cm) below the rim of the pudding basin. Adjust the amount of boiling water to suit your pot and basin.)

Gently lower the prepared pudding basin onto the trivet. Check the water level in relation to the pudding basin and adjust if necessary.

Close and lock the lid of the Instant Pot, ensuring the Pressure Valve is in the Sealing position.

Select the Steam function and set the cooking time for 120 minutes.

Once cooking time is complete allow for a complete Natural Pressure Release (Wait for the float valve to drop on it's own. This can take up to 45 minutes.)

Remove the completed pudding from the Instant Pot and carefully remove the pudding cloth and parchment paper or aluminum foil.

Allow the pudding to cool for 10-15 minutes.

Invert on a serving dish, if desired.

Serve with Bird's custard, heavy cream or ice cream.

Instant Pot Lemony Sussex Pond Pudding

Ingredients

1 recipe <u>sweet suet pastry</u> (see Page 9)
zest of 1 lemon
½ cup (45g) breadcrumbs
Filling
¾ cup (170g) cold butter, cut into small cubes
¾ cup (135g) brown sugar
1 large whole lemon, (this is a 2nd lemon with the skin intact)

Method

When making the sweet suet pastry for this recipe, add the zest of one lemon and the breadcrumbs.

Grease a 1½ quart (1.5 L) pudding basin.

Roll out the sweet suet pastry and line the pudding basin with the pastry. Reserve enough pastry to make a lid for after you have filled the pudding.

Put the lemon on a hard surface and roll it with your hand several times. This will help to release the juice. Prick the lemon all over with a fork or toothpick.

Add half the sugar, butter to the pastry-lined basin and place the whole lemon on top.

Place the remaining sugar and butter around the edge of the lemon.

Wet the edges of the suet pastry lid and place on top. Pinch the edges to seal.

Cover the top of the pudding basin with parchment paper or aluminum foil and a pudding cloth. Tie the pudding cloth securely with string and gather any excess pudding cloth over the top of the basin. Note: The pudding cloth is optional, however, you need to make sure that no water gets into the basin while it's steaming. I like to use a pudding cloth because that's the way I've always done it. And, it makes it easier to get the pudding into and out of the pot.

Place the trivet in the stainless steel liner of the Instant Pot.

Add approximately 6 cups (1.4 L) of boiling water to the inner pot (This worked perfect for the basin I used in a 6-quart Instant Pot. The goal is to have the water be about 1" (2.5 cm) below the rim of the pudding basin. Adjust the amount of boiling water to suit your pot and basin.)

Gently lower the prepared pudding basin onto the trivet. Check the water level in relation to the pudding basin and adjust if necessary.

Close and lock the lid of the Instant Pot, ensuring the Pressure Valve is in the Sealing position.

Select the Steam function and set the cooking time for 90 minutes.

Once cooking time is complete allow for a complete Natural Pressure Release (Wait for the float valve to drop on it's own. This can take up to 45 minutes.)

Remove the completed pudding from the Instant Pot and carefully remove the pudding cloth and parchment paper or aluminum foil.

Allow the pudding to cool for 10-15 minutes.

Invert on a serving dish, if desired.

Serve with Bird's custard, heavy cream or ice cream.

INSTANT POT MIDDLESEX POND PUDDING

INGREDIENTS

    1 recipe <u>sweet suet pastry</u> (see Page 9)
    zest of ½ orange
    ½ cup (45g) breadcrumbs

Filling

    1 small lemon, thinly sliced
    1 small lime, thinly sliced
    1 small orange, thinly sliced
    2 tablespoons (15g) all purpose flour
    ¾ cup (135g) brown sugar
    ½ cup (120g) cold butter, cut into small cubes

METHOD

Grease a 1½ quart (700 mL) pudding basin.

When making the sweet suet pastry for this recipe, add the orange zest and the breadcrumbs.

Roll out the sweet suet pastry and line the pudding basin with the pastry. Reserve enough pastry to make a lid for after you have filled the pudding.

In a medium bowl toss the lemon, lime and orange slices with the 2 tablespoons (15g) of all purpose flour.

To make the filling, create layers starting with 2 tablespoons (25g) of the brown sugar, 3 or 4 cubes of butter and a few slices of lemon, lime and orange. Continue with these layers until you've used up all of the filling ingredients.

Wet the edges of the suet pastry lid and place on top. Pinch the edges to seal.

Cover the top of the pudding basin with parchment paper or aluminum foil and a pudding cloth. Tie the pudding cloth securely with string and gather any excess pudding cloth over the top of the basin. Note: The pudding cloth is optional, however, you need to make sure that no water gets into the basin while it's steaming. I like to use a pudding cloth because that's the way I've always done it. And, it makes it easier to get the pudding into and out of the pot.

Place the trivet in the stainless steel liner of the Instant Pot.

Add approximately 6 cups (1.4 L) of boiling water to the inner pot (This worked perfect for the basin I used in a 6-quart Instant Pot. The goal is to have the water be about 1" (2.5 cm) below the rim of the pudding basin. Adjust the amount of boiling water to suit your pot and basin.)

Gently lower the prepared pudding basin onto the trivet. Check the water level in relation to the pudding basin and adjust if necessary.

Close and lock the lid of the Instant Pot, ensuring the Pressure Valve is in the Sealing position.

Select the Steam function and set the cooking time for 90 minutes.

Once cooking time is complete allow for a complete Natural Pressure Release (Wait for the float valve to drop on it's own. This can take up to 45 minutes.)

Remove the completed pudding from the Instant Pot and carefully remove the pudding cloth and parchment paper or aluminum foil.

Allow the pudding to cool for 10-15 minutes.

Invert on a serving dish, if desired.

Serve with Bird's custard, heavy cream or ice cream.

Instant Pot Treacle Pudding

Ingredients

¼ cup (60 mL) dark treacle, substitute molasses if you can't find treacle

¼ cup (60 mL) Tate & Lyle's golden syrup, substitute corn syrup if you can't find Tate & Lyle's

¼ teaspoon (1.25 mL) cinnamon

2 cups (240g) all purpose flour

3 teaspoons (15 mL) baking powder

1 cup (125g) suet, finely chopped (see Page 3 for alternatives)

⅓ cup (60g) brown sugar

⅓ cup (65g) white sugar

⅔ cup (160 mL) milk

2 eggs, beaten

Method

Grease a 1½ pint (700 mL) pudding basin.

Note: make sure to grease the basin well or the treacle might stick.

Pour the treacle and golden syrup into the base of the pudding basin.

In a medium bowl combine the flour, cinnamon and baking powder and mix well. Cut in the suet with a pastry blender until the mixture resembles a coarse meal.

Add both the white and brown sugar to the flour mixture and stir well.

In a medium bowl, combine the milk and beaten eggs.

Slowly pour the egg mixture into the flour mixture and stir until all ingredients are well combined and make a soft, sticky dough.

Carefully spoon the dough into the pudding basin being careful not to disturb the treacle too much.

Cover the top of the pudding basin with parchment paper or aluminum foil and a pudding cloth. Tie the pudding cloth securely with string and gather any excess pudding cloth over the top of the basin. Note: The pudding cloth is optional, however, you need to make sure that no water gets into the basin while it's steaming. I like to use a pudding cloth because that's the way I've always done it. And, it makes it easier to get the pudding into and out of the pot.

Place the trivet in the stainless steel liner of the Instant Pot.

Add approximately 6 cups (1.4 L) of boiling water to the inner pot (This worked perfect for the basin I used in a 6-quart Instant Pot. The goal is to have the water be about 1" (2.5 cm) below the rim of the pudding basin. Adjust the amount of boiling water to suit your pot and basin.)

Gently lower the prepared pudding basin onto the trivet. Check the water level in relation to the pudding basin and adjust if necessary.

Close and lock the lid of the Instant Pot, ensuring the Pressure Valve is in the Sealing position.

Select the Steam function and set the cooking time for 60 minutes.

Once cooking time is complete allow for a complete Natural Pressure Release (Wait for the float valve to drop on it's own. This can take up to 45 minutes.)

Remove the completed pudding from the Instant Pot and carefully remove the pudding cloth and parchment paper or aluminum foil.

Allow the pudding to cool on a wire rack for 5 minutes and then invert the pudding on a serving plate, allowing the treacle to dribble down the sides.

Instant Pot Cheese and Leek Suet Pudding

INGREDIENTS

1 recipe <u>savoury suet pastry</u> (see Page 8)

Filling

3 tablespoons (40g) butter
1 pound (450g) leeks
2 tablespoons (15g) all purpose flour
1 cup (100g) sharp cheddar cheese, shredded
¼ cup (60 mL) water
1 teaspoon (5 mL) dried thyme
sea salt, to taste
freshly ground black pepper, to taste

METHOD

Cut the leeks in half, lengthwise and clean well. Remove the tougher green pieces and slice.

In a large skillet, melt the butter over low heat and add the leeks. Cook for about 10 minutes or until soft. Sprinkle the flour over the leeks, mix well and continue to cook, over low heat, for another 2 minutes.

Slowly add the milk, stirring constantly. Then add the grated cheese and stir well to combine.

When the mixture begins to thicken, remove from heat and stir in the salt and pepper to taste. Set aside and allow the mixture to cool completely.

Once the cheese and leek filling has cooled, grease a 2 pint (950 mL) pudding basin, roll out the suet pastry and line the pudding basin with the pastry. Ladle the filling into the basin and then cover with a pastry lid.

Cover the top of the pudding basin with parchment paper or aluminum foil and a pudding cloth. Tie the pudding cloth securely with string and gather any excess pudding cloth over the top of the basin. Note: The pudding cloth is optional, however, you need to make sure that no water gets into the basin while it's steaming. I like to use a pudding cloth because that's the way I've always done it. And, it makes it easier to get the pudding into and out of the pot.

Place the trivet in the stainless steel liner of the Instant Pot.

Add approximately 6 cups (1.4 L) of boiling water to the inner pot (This worked perfect for the basin I used in a 6-quart Instant Pot. The goal is to have the water be about 1" (2.5 cm) below the rim of the pudding basin. Adjust the amount of boiling water to suit your pot and basin.)

Gently lower the prepared pudding basin onto the trivet. Check the water level in relation to the pudding basin and adjust if necessary.

Close and lock the lid of the Instant Pot, ensuring the Pressure Valve is in the Sealing position.

Select the Steam function and set the cooking time for 120 minutes.

Once cooking time is complete allow for a complete Natural Pressure Release (Wait for the float valve to drop on it's own. This can take up to 45 minutes.)

Remove the completed pudding from the Instant Pot and carefully remove the pudding cloth and parchment paper or aluminum foil.

Allow the pudding to cool on a wire rack for 5-10 minutes and serve.

Instant Pot Ham and Leek Suet Pudding

INGREDIENTS

    1 recipe savoury <u>suet</u> pastry (see Page 8)

Filling

    12 ounces (340g) cooked ham

    1 leek

    1½ tablespoons (25g) butter

    1½ tablespoons (11g) all purpose flour

    1 cup (240 mL) chicken stock

    2 sprigs fresh thyme

    pepper, to taste

METHOD

Cut the cooked ham into small cubes. Wash the leek well and remove the tough green top of the leek. Then cut the leek into thin slices.

In a medium saucepan, melt the butter over medium heat and cook the leek slices until tender. Sprinkle the flour over the leeks and stir well.

Slowly add the hot chicken stock, stirring constantly. Continue stirring, over medium heat, until the mixture comes to a boil and begins to thicken.

Reduce heat and add the thyme, cream and ham.

Stir well and simmer for about 5 minutes.

Remove from heat and set aside to cool.

Once the ham and leek filling has cooled, grease a 2 pint (950 mL) pudding basin, roll out the suet pastry and line the pudding basin with the pastry. Ladle the filling into the basin and then cover with a pastry lid.

Cover the top of the pudding basin with parchment paper or aluminum foil and a pudding cloth. Tie the pudding cloth securely with string and gather any excess pudding cloth over the top of the basin. Note: The pudding cloth is optional, however, you need to make sure that no water gets into the basin while it's steaming. I like to use a pudding cloth because that's the way I've always done it. And, it makes it easier to get the pudding into and out of the pot.

Place the trivet in the stainless steel liner of the Instant Pot.

Add approximately 6 cups (1.4 L) of boiling water to the inner pot (This worked perfect for the basin I used in a 6-quart Instant Pot. The goal is to have the water be about 1" (2.5 cm) below the rim of the pudding basin. Adjust the amount of boiling water to suit your pot and basin.)

Gently lower the prepared pudding basin onto the trivet. Check the water level in relation to the pudding basin and adjust if necessary.

Close and lock the lid of the Instant Pot, ensuring the Pressure Valve is in the Sealing position.

Select the Steam function and set the cooking time for 60 minutes.

Once cooking time is complete allow for a complete Natural Pressure Release (Wait for the float valve to drop on it's own. This can take up to 45 minutes.)

Remove the completed pudding from the Instant Pot and carefully remove the pudding cloth and parchment paper or aluminum foil.

Allow the pudding to cool for 10-15 minutes.

Invert on a serving dish, if desired.

Instant Pot Steak and Kidney Pudding

Making The Filling

The filling of a steak and kidney pudding is actually a steak and kidney stew. The Instant Pot excels at stew and with this recipe you will be sure to make the best beef stew you have ever tasted. Save what won't fit in your pudding basin to add to the pudding as you serve or freeze it and serve another day as stew.

Ingredients

   3 pounds (1.5 Kg) blade or top sirloin roast, cut into
   ¾ - 1 inch (2 - 2.5 cm) cubes
   1 large onion, cut in bite size pieces
   3 - 4 large carrots, cut into 1 inch (2.5 cm) pieces
   1 tablespoon (15 mL) Bovril™
   1 teaspoon (5 mL) salt, or to taste
   Stock to just cover
   3 ounces (85g) beef kidney, cut into 6 pieces (optional
   but recommended)
   2 teaspoons (10 mL) cornstarch (or sufficient)

Method

Dust the beef and kidney with unbleached all purpose flour.

Press the Sauté key on the Instant Pot and add the beef and kidney to the stainless steel inner pot, stirring vigorously to prevent the meat from sticking.

When the meat is seared, pour in just enough stock to cover the meat.

   Don't add too much liquid as you'll dilute the taste

Add the carrots, onions, Bovril™ and salt.

Close the lid and turn the vent to Sealing

Click the Meat/Stew button add set the time to 30 minutes.

When the time is up Quick release to vent the steam

Mix the cornstarch with just enough water to make it liquid and stir it into the stew. If the stew doesn't thicken you may have to turn on Sauté for a few minutes to bring to simmer while stirring.

The gravy should have the consistency of cooking oil.

PUDDING INGREDIENTS

1 recipe <u>savoury suet pastry</u> (see Page 8)
3 - 4 cups (700 - 900 mL) of the Steak & Kidney filling from the previous page.
¼ cup (60 mL) of the gravy from the stew

METHOD

Grease a 2 pint (950 mL) pudding basin.

Roll out the suet pastry, using ¾ of the pastry for the lining and ¼ for lid.

Line the pudding basin with the pastry and gently ladle the filling into the basin.

Use a slotted spoon to avoid putting too much liquid in the pudding which will make the pastry mushy.

Make sure the filling is cold or at least cool.

The basin should be almost full with the drained filling.

Add ¼ cup (60 mL) of the reserved gravy to the filling.

Carefully add the pastry lid and pinch all around the edge to seal it.

Cover the top of the pudding with parchment paper or aluminum foil and a pudding cloth.

Tie the pudding cloth securely with string and gather any excess pudding cloth over the top of the basin.

Note: The pudding cloth is optional, however, you need to make sure that no water gets into the basin while it's steaming. I like to use a pudding cloth because that's the way I've always done it. And, it makes it easier to get the pudding into and out of the pot.

Place the trivet in the stainless steel liner of the Instant Pot.

Add approximately 6 cups (1.4 L) of boiling water to the inner pot (This worked for the basin I used in a 6 quart (6 litre) Instant Pot.

The goal is to have the water be about 1" (2.5 cm) below the rim of the pudding basin. Adjust the amount of boiling water to suit your pot and basin.)

Gently lower the prepared pudding basin onto the trivet. Check the water level in relation to the pudding basin and adjust if necessary.

Close and lock the lid of the Instant Pot, ensuring the Pressure Valve is in the Sealing position.

Select the Steam function and set the cooking time for 45 minutes.

Once cooking time is complete allow for a complete Natural Pressure Release (Wait for the float valve to drop on it's own. This can take up to 45 minutes.)

Remove the completed pudding from the Instant Pot and carefully remove the pudding cloth and parchment paper or aluminum foil.

Allow the pudding to cool for 5 - 10 minutes.

Note: This pudding should be served directly from the basin, not turned out onto a plate.

Serve the pudding with the rest of the gravy (reheated separately), boiled potatoes and fresh peas or scarlet runner beans.

BONUS ~ Claim Your Free Book

Thank you for buying this book! As a bonus we would like to give you another one absolutely free - No Strings Attached

You can choose any of the books in our catalog as your bonus. Just use this link or scan the QR code below -

https://fun.geezerguides.com/freebook

PLEASE REVIEW

As independent publishers, we rely on reviews and word-of-mouth recommendations to get the word out about our books.

If you've enjoyed this book, please consider leaving a review at the website you purchased it from

IF YOU'RE NOT SATISFIED

We aspire to the highest standards with all our books. If, for some reason, you're not satisfied, please let us know and we will try to make it right. You can always return the book for a full refund but we hope you will reserve that as a last option.

ABOUT THE AUTHOR

Geoff Wells was born in a small town outside London, England just after the 2nd World War. He left home at sixteen and emigrated to Canada, settling in the Toronto area of Southern Ontario. He had many jobs and interests early in life from real estate sales to helicopter pilot to restaurant owner. When the personal computer era began he finally settled down and became a computer programmer until he took early retirement. Now, as an author, he has written several popular series including: Authentic English Recipes, Reluctant Vegetarians and Terra Novian Reports, to name a few. He and his wife (and oft times co-author), Vicky, have been married since 1988 and divide their time between Ontario, Canada and the island of Eleuthera in The Bahamas.

Find all of Geoff's books at

https://ebooks.geezerguides.com

Follow Geoff on social media

 https://facebook.com/AuthorGeoffWells/

 geoffwells@ebooks.geezerguides.com

ABOUT OUR COOKBOOKS

QUALITY

We are passionate about producing quality cookbooks. You'll never find "cut and pasted" recipes in any of our books.

CONSISTENCY

We endeavor to create consistent methods for both ingredients and instructions. In most of our recipes, the ingredients will be listed in the order in which they are used. We also try to make sure that the instructions make sense, are clear and are arranged in a logical order.

ONLY QUALITY INGREDIENTS

To ensure that all of our recipes turn out exactly right, we call for only fresh, quality ingredients. You'll never find "ingredients" such as cake mixes, artificial sweeteners, artificial egg replacements, or any pre-packaged items. Ingredients, to us, are items in their natural (or as close to natural as possible), singular form: eggs, milk, cream, flour, salt, sugar, butter, coconut oil, vanilla extract, etc.

ENGLISH SPEAKING AUTHORS

We write all our books ourselves and never outsource them or scrape content from the Internet.

FOUND AN ERROR?

Although we do our best to make sure everything is accurate and complete, mistakes happen.

If you've found an error - a missing ingredient, an incorrect measurement, a temperature that's wrong, etc. - please let us know so we can correct it.

Just e-mail us at oops@geezerguides.com and we'll make any necessary corrections.

Published by Geezer Guides

When you see *Published by Geezer Guides* on any book, you can be confident that you are purchasing a quality product.

About Geezer Guides

Geezer Guides is a small independent publisher that only publishes original manuscripts. We will never sell you something that has just been copied from the Internet. All our books are properly formatted with a clickable table of contents.

Other Books You May Like

You can find our complete catalog at

https://ebooks.geezerguides.com

Plus Many More

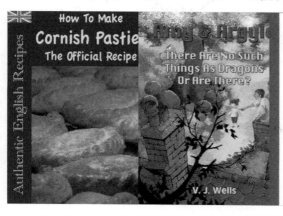

Plus Many More

Printed in Great Britain
by Amazon

63857058R00047